AF407125

The Self I Was Yet to Know

Shannon Xireille

Copyright © 2026 Shannon Xireille

All rights reserved.

ISBN: 979-8-9944397-3-9

DEDICATION

. . .to the bearer of lineage & the bridge between our ancestry & our future.

Mommy & her oldest three – by grace, love & legacy.

CONTENTS

ACKNOWLEDGMENTS

This book is the result of a long and tender healing journey—one shaped by courage, reflection, and the willingness to confront both pain and growth. I first acknowledge myself, for choosing to heal even when it was uncomfortable, and for honoring the process rather than rushing the outcome.

I want to acknowledge not only those who stayed, but also those who walked away.

Your absence became one of my greatest teachers. Through you, I learned how to love myself more deeply. I learned that walking away from someone is not always an act of rejection, but sometimes an act of protection—for yourself, and for them.

You taught me the meaning of boundaries when none had existed before. You showed me independence by leaving me to stand on my own. And in your departure, you gave me the gift of accountability—the ability to look inward, to grow, and to take responsibility for who I was becoming.

Though our paths no longer align, your impact remains.
For the lessons, the growth, and the strength that followed,
I acknowledge you with gratitude.

I acknowledge the teachers, mentors, and experiences -
both gentle and challenging - that guided me toward deeper
self-awareness and understanding. Each lesson, whether
learned through love or adversity, contributed to the
wisdom reflected in these pages.

May these pages offer connection, comfort, and permission
for others to begin or continue their own healing journeys.

Part I | The Hurt

There was a time when I believed
I had to erase the woman I used to be
in order to become the woman I wanted to be.
I thought healing meant disowning her -
the girl who loved too deeply,
trusted too easily,
stayed too long,
believed too hard,
broke too quietly.

I tried to outrun her.
Rewrite her.
Replace her.
Bury her.

But healing revealed something truer.
She was never my enemy.
She was my beginning.
My foundation.
My becoming.

She lived in survival,
in longing,
in silence,
in fear.

She carried heartbreak like a backpack
and shame like a second skin.
She kept loving people
who didn't know how to love her back
because she didn't yet know
how to love herself first.

She accepted crumbs
because she didn't know
there was a feast inside her.

She stayed where she was minimized
because no one had taught her
how to multiply herself.

She broke down
because she didn't know
she was allowed to rebuild.

But she wasn't weak.
She was wounded.
And wounded women are not to be mocked—
Or always understood, but respected.

She learned everything the hurting version of her,
never had the chance to learn.

She learned that peace is a responsibility.
That love without boundaries is self-abandonment.
That forgiveness does not require reconciliation.
That accountability is a gift.
That soft living is not luxury—
it is alignment.
That God was not far—
she just wasn't listening.

She learned to sit with silence
instead of fearing it.
She learned to choose herself
instead of begging to be chosen.
She learned to love gently
without losing strength,
and love boldly
without losing self-respect.

She learned that when God removes something,
He is not punishing.
He is protecting.

She learned the language of peace.
She learned the posture of trust.
She learned the cost of availability.
She learned the power of identity.

She learned responsibility,
truth,
clarity,
wisdom,
discernment.

She learned to walk away
without collapsing.

She learned to heal
and still be whole
in the places she once broke.

CHAPTER I

DIRE LEGITIMACY

I have spent years chasing the woman I thought I
needed to become.

The future version of me who was stronger, softer,
wiser, healed.

But in the sprint toward who I wanted to be, I
abandoned the girl who was already here.
The one who held the scars, the memories, the truth.
The one who needed me most.

I'm sorry, baby.
I'm sorry I left you behind.
I'm sorry I believed them when they said you were
weak.
I'm sorry I let the world teach me to fear you, hide you,
criticize you.
I betrayed you in ways that didn't look like betrayal.
Not the kind people whisper about—
but the quiet kind.

The kind that looks like choosing everyone else first.
The kind that looks like shrinking to fit inside other people's
comfort.
The kind that looks like giving yourself away piece by
painful piece.

I was unfaithful to myself
long before I ever expected faithfulness from others.

I stepped outside my own home -
emotionally, mentally, physically, spiritually -
every time I placed someone else's needs above my own
and called it love.

Every time I handed someone access to places in me
they never earned the right to enter.
Every time I believed their voice over mine.
I thought self-sacrifice made me good.
But all it did was make me absent.

Disconnected.

Cold.

A stranger to my own heart.

There were parts of me I refused to come home to
because I feared what I would find there:
the grief I buried,
the tenderness I abandoned,
the innocence I let others destroy.

And yet -
    the truth has a way of bleeding through the cracks
    of every version of yourself you try to pretend to be.
    It spills into your relationships,
    your choices,
    your silence,
    your reflection.

    It waits for you patiently
    until you finally whisper,
    "I'm ready."

I used to think healing meant overlooking what hurt me.
Now I know healing meant finally seeing what I had done
to myself.

I neglected the girl who only ever wanted my protection.
I silenced the girl who only ever wanted to be believed.
I abandoned the girl who still waited for me
long after everyone else walked away.

So this chapter is not a confession of weakness,
it is a confession of return.

A vow to the girl I left behind:
I see you now.
I hear you now.
I believe you now.

And I will not leave you again.
The truths that bled through my life were never out to
destroy me.
They were trying to guide me back home.

Home to myself.

CHAPTER 2

THE GARDEN BENEATH MY GRIEF

There is a garden beneath every wound,
a landscape we pretend not to see -
roots tangled in memory,
soil heavy with the weight of everything we never said out
loud.

My grief had a voice long before I ever learned to listen to
it.
She whispered from the corners of my silence,
from the shadows behind my strength,
from the places I kept hidden even from myself.

Her voice sounded like accusation at first:

How dare you let them treat us like that.
How dare you call pain "loyalty."
How dare you abandon me, too.
Your loyalty to them was your desertion of me.

I didn't realize she wasn't angry at the world,
she was angry at me.
Because I kept choosing everyone else's comfort
over my own survival.

She asked me questions I didn't want to answer:

Why wasn't I good enough for you?
Why do you praise everyone else but refuse to see me?
Why did you leave me for people who never stayed for you?

It is one thing to be unloved by others.
It is another to be unloved by yourself.

That kind of grief is not loud.
It is quiet, patient,
the kind that grows in the space between who you were
and who you pretended to be.

It blooms slowly, painfully,
with petals of guilt
and thorns of confusion.

There were parts of me that waited for years
for a kind word from my own mouth.
Parts that wanted to tell me,
I think your smile is beautiful, but knew I wouldn't believe
it.
Parts that missed me even while I lived inside my own skin.
Parts that longed to be fought for.

Grief became the friend I never meant to invite in the one
who refused to leave until I faced her fully.

I didn't understand then
that grief is not the enemy.
She is the guardian of the truth.

She reveals where you abandoned yourself.
She exposes who you pretended to be.
She uncovers the burial grounds of your self-worth.

And when she is done breaking you open,
she hands you seeds.

The garden beneath my grief taught me this:
What you do not confront, you repeat.
What you do not honor, you lose.
What you do not love, you eventually destroy.

My grief didn't want vengeance.
She wanted honesty.
She wanted presence.
She wanted me.

And when I finally stopped running long enough to listen,
she said the words I had been avoiding for years:

"You weren't invisible.
You were ignored.
There is a difference.
And now that I know my worth,
I choose absence over invisibility."

Her voice – my voice -
stopped begging to be chosen
and started choosing herself.

The breaking was never the ending.
It was the planting.

And I am no longer ashamed
of what had to die
so that I could grow

Chapter 3

THE SILENCE THAT FOLLOWED

Silence is not always peaceful.
Sometimes it is the echo of everything you tried to outrun.

Sometimes it is the room you trap yourself in
because the truth is too loud everywhere else.

After the grief came the quiet -
not the soft kind,
not the healing kind,
but the kind that makes you question your own voice.

I didn't trust myself anymore.
I didn't trust my heart,
my desires,
my judgment,
my ability to choose anyone
including me.

I had loved the wrong people so deeply
that I began to believe love itself was the problem.
That perhaps I wasn't meant for the kind of affection I
offered so freely.

That maybe the softness in me was a flaw
and the tenderness I carried was a liability.

In the silence, I asked questions
I didn't want the answers to:

Who am I if I'm not who everyone needs me to be?
If I stop pouring into them, will anyone pour into me?
If I stop showing up, will anyone even notice I'm gone?

And the silence answered honestly.
Brutally.
Repeatedly.

It told me that the people I bent myself to reach
wouldn't bend an inch to reach me.
It showed me that I was loyal to those
who were merely entertained by my presence.
It revealed that the love I gave so abundantly
was rarely reciprocated with intention.

Silence exposed every illusion I tried to cradle.
Including the one where I believed
I could love someone into loving me.

That belief kept me small.
Quiet.
Over giving.
Invisible.

I thought shrinking made me safer.

I thought lowering my expectations meant I wouldn't feel
the sting of rejection.

I thought if I didn't ask for titles, loyalty, clarity, or
accountability,

I wouldn't feel disappointed when they didn't offer them.

But silence has a way of telling the truth
even when you don't want to hear it:

People treat you how they feel about you.
And you allow it based on how you feel about yourself.

Silence made me confront the way I hid my worth
behind performance.
Behind loyalty.
Behind caretaking.
Behind surviving.

I realized I believed others more than I believed myself.
I trusted their attention more than I trusted my intuition.

I trusted their presence more than I trusted God's protection.

In the quiet, I also saw how often I apologized for existing.
How often I tried to fix things that were never mine to carry.

How often I made myself small
so no one would feel threatened by my softness,
my intelligence,
my beauty,
my resilience.

But silence is a teacher.
Not a kind one—
but an honest one.

If affection is not freely given,
I don't want it.
If love requires me to abandon myself,
it is not love.
If I must break myself to be chosen,
I refuse to be an option.
If I must lose my voice to keep the peace,
then peace was never present.

And perhaps the hardest truth. . .

I wasn't afraid of being alone.
I was afraid of being alone with me.

Because being alone with me
meant facing the truth that I had become someone
I didn't recognize -
someone who didn't love herself enough
to stay loyal to her own heart.

But even in the silence,
God whispered:

"I never asked you to be perfect.
I asked you to be honest."

And honesty,
slowly, painfully,
began to pull me out of the quiet.

The silence that followed wasn't punishment.
It was the mirror.
It was the reset.
It was the place where the girl I abandoned
waited for me to come home.

And this time,
I listened

Chapter 4

PARENTAL WOUNDS

Heartbreaks are not exclusive to romance.

Some can be romantic, familial, organizational and occupational, friendship based . . .

The nonromantic ones shaped the way I loved.

The kind you inherit before you even understand what love is.
The kind that whispers its wounds into every relationship and association afterward.
The kind you grow up calling "normal."

My father was my first unanswered question.
My first lesson in absence.
My first contradiction -
a man I longed for
and a man I learned to live without.

As a child, I thought his distance was something I earned.
As an adult, I realized it was something he chose.

But the wound didn't begin with his leaving.
It began with the way I defended him.

The way I gave him the benefit of every doubt
at the expense of my own clarity.

The way I created a fantasy of who he was
because the truth was too heavy for a little girl to hold.

I convinced myself he was good,
misunderstood,
wounded,
a victim of circumstance -
anything to avoid admitting
that he simply wasn't who I needed him to be.

I didn't realize I had inherited a habit:
romanticizing the bare minimum.

From him, I learned how to hope for scraps
and call them blessings.
How to tolerate inconsistency
and call it effort.
How to excuse mistreatment
and call it love.

He taught me - without meaning to -
how to love emotionally unavailable people.
How to chase validation.
How to accept crumbs because at least crumbs meant
something.
How to confuse attention with affection
and manipulation with intimacy.

When we finally connected later in life,
I thought the healing would begin.
Instead, the wound finally spoke.

His lies didn't just distort my name -
they distorted my reflection.
He painted versions of me that never existed.
He spoke words about me that I never deserved.
He told stories about my mother that weren't rooted in truth
but control.

And still, I came back.
Still, I tried.
Still, I believed in his potential more than I believed the
reality.

Healing wasn't about forgiving him.
Forgiveness is easy for me.
Healing was about finally believing myself
over him.

One day, I realized:
I wasn't trying to protect him.
I was trying to protect the little girl in me
who needed her father to be good
so she could believe she was worthy of good things.

But the truth is not cruel-
it is clarifying.

He showed me who he was.
I was the one who refused to see it.

He wasn't the villain.
He wasn't the victim.
He was simply a man.
A man whose limitations shaped my childhood.
A man whose absence trained me to overstay in places
where love was inconsistent, and conditions were many.
A man whose version of love
taught me what love was not.

And acknowledging that truth
wasn't an act of betrayal-
it was an act of freedom.

I stopped romanticizing potential.
I stopped accepting the bare minimum.
I stopped confusing effort with excuses.
I stopped letting people call me ungrateful
for craving the love I deserved.

The father wound didn't close when he apologized-
it closed when I stopped abandoning myself
to hold the door open for someone who kept walking away.

I realized I didn't hate him.
I didn't resent him.
I didn't wish him harm.
I simply chose to no longer carry a relationship
that lived on life support.

The girl in me cried when I made that choice.
The woman in me stood up straighter.

Some people break your heart
to keep you from breaking yourself later.

He was the first man to teach me what disappointment felt
like.
But God made sure he wasn't the last man
to teach me what resilience looks like.

I forgive him.
But forgiveness does not require participation.
Closure does not require proximity.
And love does not require suffering.

I release him.
I release the story I told myself about him.
I release the weight that was never mine to carry.

The father wound no longer defines me.
It refined me

Chapter 5

THE PATTERNS THAT BROKE ME

Some patterns don't look like destruction at first.
They look like survival.
They look like coping.
They look like "doing the best I can."
Until one day you realize
you've built a life out of habits
that were only meant to get you through a moment.

Pain taught me routines I never questioned.
Heartbreak taught me behaviors I normalized.
Exhaustion taught me standards I settled into
because I didn't have the strength to expect more.

The hardest part of healing
is recognizing the ways you contributed
to your own suffering.
Not because you deserved it,
but because brokenness becomes familiar-
and familiarity becomes home
even when it hurts.

Weight of the Heart, Weight on the Body

My weight didn't change because I was lazy.
My weight changed because heartbreak is heavy.
Because grief sits inside the bones
long after it leaves the room.
Because emotional exhaustion
steals energy from the body
until all you have left is survival.

I wasn't overeating-
I was overwhelmed.
I wasn't unmotivated-
I was undone.
Every pound became a record of a moment
where I poured into someone else
when I had nothing left for myself.

Robbing Peter to Pay Paul

Financial chaos was another pattern
I pretended wasn't a pattern.

I told myself I "deserved a break,"
"deserved to treat myself,"
"deserved to escape."
But the truth was simple:
I was trying to buy moments of peace
because I didn't know how to create it.

It wasn't the nails, the hair, the trips,
the little purchases of temporary joy-
it was the lie behind them:
"I'll fix my life later."

Later never came.
Because running from responsibility
is a habit that feels easier
than facing the consequences of neglect.

And I had become an expert at self-neglect.

Emotional Loops

I kept placing myself in situations
I had prayed my way out of.
I kept returning to versions of myself
I swore I buried.
I kept engaging with people
whose behavior I had already healed from.

Healing isn't linear,
but my patterns weren't setbacks-
they were cycles.
Cycles built on:

over giving

under receiving

silencing myself

romanticizing inconsistency

accepting apologies without change

mistaking attention for affection

I thought loyalty meant endurance.
I thought patience meant self-sacrifice.
I thought giving chances meant maturity.
But all it meant was this:
I didn't yet believe I deserved more.

The Quiet Sabotage

Self-sabotage isn't loud.
It's gentle.
It shows up in the choices you postpone,
the boundaries you avoid enforcing,
the goals you delay,
the energy you ignore.

Mine sounded like:
"I'll start tomorrow."
"It's not that bad."
"At least I'm trying."
"They didn't mean it."
"I can handle it."

And I could handle it-
until handling it became my identity.

The Breaking Point

Every pattern eventually asks for payment.
Mine asked for:

my peace

my clarity

my self-respect

my confidence

my joy

my time

my body

my voice

And for a while,
I paid it willingly.
Because I thought suffering was the price of love.
Because I thought endurance was a virtue.
Because I thought pain proved my worth.

But the truth is simple:

Nothing that requires you to abandon yourself
will ever be worth keeping.

The patterns that broke me
were also the patterns that revealed me.
They made one thing undeniably clear:

I wasn't weak-
I was wounded.
And wounds repeat themselves
until they are healed.

This chapter is not about shame.
It is about understanding.
Because understanding is the first step
toward breaking what once broke you.

And in the breaking of those patterns,
I began to shape the woman.

Part II | The Awakening

Chapter 6

CHOOSING PEACE OVER CHAOS

Peace was not the gentle place I imagined.
It was not soft music and slow mornings.
It was not a candlelit room or a quiet mind.
Peace, for me, began as a confrontation-
a reckoning with the chaos I had grown comfortable in.

For years, chaos felt like home.
Not because I wanted turmoil,
but because I understood it.
It matched the rhythm of my childhood,
the tone of my relationships,
the pattern of my self-worth.
Chaos didn't scare me-
stability did.

Stability required presence.
Presence required honesty.
And honesty required admitting
that the life I had built
was louder than the life I needed.

Choosing peace meant walking away
from what was familiar
to step into what was foreign.

Peace Is My Responsibility

I used to say,
"I just want someone to be my peace."

But the truth was simple:
I didn't know how to be at peace with myself.
And so I placed the burden of my healing
on people who were never meant to carry it.

No partner, no friend, no relationship
was created to fix what I refused to face.
Peace was not something anyone could give me.
It was something I had to build-
piece by piece, boundary by boundary,
truth by truth.

I stopped expecting others to calm storms
I continued to walk into.
I stopped asking for gentleness
in spaces where I did not set the tone.
I stopped burdening people
with responsibilities that belonged to me.

Privacy Is Protection

There is peace in closing the door
before the world enters the room.
Not secrecy - discernment.
Not isolation - intention.

Healing taught me that my life
does not need to be consumed
to be understood.
That silence is not loneliness -
it is clarity.
That privacy is not distance -
it is alignment.

Not everyone deserves access
to the unfiltered versions of me.
Not everyone earns the right
to witness my growth.
Not everyone is safe enough
to hold my truth.

Peace is sometimes the decision
to let people wonder
instead of letting them wound.

Refusing to Match Energy

People told me,
"Match their energy."
But I learned that matching energy
is a dangerous imitation.

I refuse to mirror demons
just to prove I see them.
I refuse to become hard
to show I am unbreakable.
I refuse to degrade myself
to speak a language
I never want to be fluent in.

If peace requires my silence,
I will be quiet.
If peace requires my departure,
I will leave.
If peace requires restraint,
I will hold myself firm.

Matching energy is easy.
Maintaining integrity is mastery.

Peace Requires Boundaries

Boundaries were the first sign that I was choosing myself.
Not selfishness -self-respect.
Not fear -clarity.

Boundaries gave me:

room to breathe

space to think

time to feel

the right to say no

the permission to stop explaining myself

the strength to walk away

the discernment to choose differently

Peace arrived the moment
I stopped negotiating with myself
to keep others comfortable.

The Cost of Chaos

Chaos cost me years of energy.
It stole sleep, joy, money, opportunities,
and pieces of myself I can never get back.

Peace cost me people.
People who benefited from my lack of boundaries,
people who loved the version of me
who didn't love herself enough to say no,
people who preferred me overwhelmed
because it made me easier to control.

Losing them felt like grief-
until I realized losing them
was gaining me.

Choosing Peace Every Day

Peace is not a destination-
it is a discipline.
A choice I make
every morning,
every moment,
every time my past tries to pull me back.

Chaos is loud.
Peace is quiet.
But in the quiet,
I finally hear myself.

I am no longer seduced by storms.
I no longer crave what hurts me.
I no longer return to what kept me broken.

Peace is the woman I am becoming.
Peace is the life I am building.
Peace is the home I am returning to
every time I choose myself.

Chapter 7

ACCOUNTABILITY FOR IDENTITY

Accountability is not punishment.
It is alignment.
It is truth meeting action.
It is the bridge between who you were
and who you are becoming.

But before accountability can reshape you,
it must first confront you.
Not gently.
Not softly.
Not with the language of comfort-
but with the clarity of truth.

Healing required me to stop explaining my pain
and start examining my patterns.
To stop justifying my decisions
and start understanding them.
To stop blaming circumstances
and start asking myself real questions:

Why did I allow that?
Why didn't I walk away?
Why did I betray myself to keep someone else?
Why did I abandon my standards for temporary affection?

And most painfully:
Why was I so afraid of the truth?

The Four Lies We Live

There are four places where lies are born-
not from malice,
but from identity.
From who we think we are
and who we fear we are not.

1. When you don't know who you are, you live a lie.
Identity becomes performance.
You shape yourself into whatever the world praises
and lose the blueprint of your own soul.

2. When you won't face your truth, you tell lies.
The lies sound like excuses,
but they're really fear in disguise.

3. When you won't accept your truth, you deepen the lie.
You reject accountability
because you're terrified that accepting the truth
means admitting you are flawed,
human,
wounded.

4. When you reject your truth, you become the lie.
You lose the original version of yourself
beneath layers of pretending.

Identity without honesty is just a costume.

Facing Myself Was the Hardest Part

I used to think accountability meant guilt.
Blame.
Punishment.
Shame.

But true accountability is none of these.

Accountability is self-respect in action.
It is saying:
"I deserve better,
and I will become better,
starting with me."

It looks like:

admitting what you allowed

acknowledging what you ignored

accepting what you enabled

understanding what you repeated

and choosing differently.

I realized I wasn't a victim of circumstance-
I was a victim of my own silence.
I kept the door open for the same people
who kept walking through me.
I stayed in places
where I was shrinking
just to be tolerated.
I held onto situations
God was trying to free me from.

Accountability was not the enemy.
It was the invitation.

Identity Built on Truth

Identity is not who the world says you are,
who your trauma shaped you to be,
or who you had to become to survive.

Identity is who you choose to be
once survival is no longer your only language.

I used to say,
"I don't know who I am."
But healing revealed the truth:
I always knew.
I just didn't believe she was enough.

The real me was quiet beneath the noise.
Soft beneath the armor.
Honest beneath the performance.
Present beneath the fear.

She wasn't missing—
she was muted.
Buried beneath the lies I lived
to make other people comfortable.

The Courage to Accept Responsibility

Accountability without change
is manipulation.
Accountability without growth
is stagnation.
Accountability without humility
is self-deception.

But accountability with intention
is transformation.

The moment I said,
"Yes, that was me-
but it is not me anymore,"
I stepped into a new identity.
Not the fantasy version of myself
I chased for years,
but the healed version
I am now becoming.

The Truth That Freed Me

The why behind my wrong
did not excuse the behavior.
But it did explain the wound.
And when I understood the wound,
I finally understood myself.

Identity is not defined by what broke you.
It is defined by who you become
after you choose to stop breaking yourself.

Accountability gave me permission
to rewrite my story-
not from pain,
but from truth.

And truth,
when finally welcomed,
is the birthplace of becoming.

Chapter 8

SOFT LIVING IS SELF CARE

Softness was never something I grew up trusting.
Softness felt dangerous-
too open,
too vulnerable,
too exposed.
In a world where hardness was rewarded
and composure was applauded,
softness felt like a luxury
I did not believe I had earned.

But healing revealed something I never expected:
Softness wasn't weakness.
Softness was wisdom.
Softness was protection.
Softness was strength that no longer needed to shout.

Soft living was not about wealth,
luxury,
or aesthetics.
It was not spa days or designer rituals
or curated moments for the sake of appearance.

Soft living, for me,
was a spiritual decision.
A lifestyle of gentleness-
not because life became easier,
but because I finally stopped making it harder for myself.

Soft Living Is Emotional Clarity

I used to associate "soft" with materialism-
pretty things,
pretty places,
pretty illusions.
But the softness I craved
had nothing to do with what money could buy.

Soft living was:

letting go of chaos

releasing the urge to fix everyone

protecting my peace

speaking kindly to myself

refusing to live in survival mode

creating quiet in a loud world

Softness began the day I realized
I didn't need to defend myself
to be understood
nor destroy myself
to be loved.

Self-Care Without a Price Tag

The world sells self-care
as if healing requires a receipt.
But the most transformative kinds of care
cost nothing- only intention.

Self-care looked like:

going to bed when I was tired

drinking water before I spiraled

cleaning my space so my mind could breathe

taking a walk when my thoughts got loud

saying "no" without guilt

disconnecting from conversations that drained me

being honest about how I felt

letting myself rest without earning it

The softest thing I ever did
was stop punishing myself
for needing what I needed.

Seeking God as a Form of Self-Love

There came a moment when I realized
I wasn't just exhausted-
I was spiritually malnourished.
I wanted peace
but I didn't seek the One
who created it.

Spending time with God
became the most intimate form of self-care I had ever
known.
Prayer became my grounding.
Scripture became my mirror.
Stillness became my healing.

When I apologized to God
for letting money, pain, fear, and people
become idols in my life,
I wasn't confessing to be punished-
I was confessing to come home.

Softness was returning to the truth
that I didn't need to manipulate life
to receive what God already intended for me.

Letting Go of Hardness

I used to wear hardness
like armor.
Like identity.
Like survival.

But hardness was not strength;
it was fear wearing steel.

Hardness said:
"I won't let you hurt me."
Softness said:
"I trust myself enough to walk away if you try."

Hardness said:
"I must be loud to be heard."
Softness said:
"My peace will speak for me."

Hardness said:
"I have to earn love."
Softness said:
"I deserve love without performance."

The woman I am becoming
no longer confuses walls with boundaries, silence with
strength, or emotional distance with maturity.

Soft Living Does Not Depend on Anyone Else

Softness is not about a partner.
Not about finances.
Not about lifestyle upgrades.

Softness is internal.
It is cultivated, not purchased.
It is chosen, not given.
It is maintained, not requested.

Soft living costs:

your pride

your defensiveness

your fear

your toxic comforts

your need for control

your attachment to chaos

The reward is:

peace

presence

clarity

intimacy

grace

self-respect

The Softest Version of Me Is the Strongest Version of Me

Soft living didn't make me weaker-
it made me whole.
It taught me how to breathe in rooms
where I once suffocated.
How to be gentle in moments
where I once spiraled.
How to walk away from what hurt me
without needing permission or apology.

I stopped chasing peace
in people and places
that were never designed to hold it.

I became the peace.
I became the softness.
I became the calm I once begged for.

Soft living was not a phase.
It was a homecoming.
A return to the woman
God always knew I was-
beneath the armor,
beneath the fear,
beneath the chaos.

Chapter 9

THE COST OF AVAILABILITY

Availability is a currency.
One more expensive than money,
more draining than labor,
more revealing than words.

For years, I gave my availability away
like it was free-
as if time replenished itself,
as if my energy had no limits,
as if my presence was an endless resource
for anyone who needed it.

But availability is not abundance.
It is sacrifice.
It costs something every single time.

Time Is Not Just Time

Time is emotional labor.
It is mental bandwidth.
It is spiritual capacity.
It is the quiet energy required
to be present with someone
even when you're not at peace yourself.

People ask for time
with no idea what it withdraws from you.

They want more of your presence
without understanding
that presence requires pieces-
pieces of your mind,
your patience,
your heart,
your energy.

Some people ask for hours
when they have not earned a minute.
Some want access
without investment.
Some expect you to be "available"
even when they have never been responsible
with the access they already had.

The Expense of Emotional Availability

Being emotionally available
cost me the most.

It cost me:

sleep

clarity

boundaries

mental peace

physical energy

spiritual alignment

my own needs

my own healing

I learned this the hard way:
Some people do not want your presence -
they want your capacity.
They want the emotional labor
you perform so naturally
because they do not know how
to hold themselves.

I thought generosity was love.
I thought endurance was loyalty.
I thought accessibility was kindness.

But true kindness is balanced.
True generosity is reciprocal.
True loyalty does not drain you dry.

What Men and Women Often Forget

I learned to observe what people require of me
and what they offer in return -
not in bitterness,
but in truth.

If a man desires a soft, calm, feminine woman,
he must understand
that softness requires protection,
and calm requires stability.
A woman cannot be peaceful
in an environment that is chaotic.

If a woman desires a masculine, leading man,
she must understand
that leadership requires space,
and respect requires trust.
A man cannot lead a woman
who is still fighting the battles
of her past relationships.

Availability is not just time together-
it is the cost of what each person must give up
to create a safe environment
for connection, intimacy, and peace.

If a man wants a stay-at-home wife,
he must carry the weight
of an entire household.
Not because she is incapable-
but because her availability is a form of currency
that allows him to operate in his purpose
without fear of collapse at home.

If a woman wants to be cherished,
she must enter a place of vulnerability
that requires the death of pride,
ego,
and being "hard" for protection.

Both availability and intimacy
require sacrifice.

The Price of Overextending Yourself

If you constantly offer your availability
to those who drain you,
you will have nothing left
for those who deserve you.

If you continue to say yes out of guilt,
you will resent the very people
you are trying to please.

If you keep being emotionally present
for people who never show up,
you will forget what it feels like
to be cared for.

I learned to stop giving access
to those who only understood my availability
as convenience
rather than privilege.

People who treat you like an option
should not have the luxury
of your consistency.

The Value of Withholding Access

I used to fear being unavailable.
I thought absence would push people away.
I thought distance made me unlovable.
I thought saying "not today"
made me difficult.

Now I understand something simple:
Withholding access is how you reclaim your worth.

I am not always available.
I am not always reachable.
I am not always accessible.
My time must be earned.
My presence must be respected.
My energy must be protected.

Because the healed version of me
knows this truth deeply:

When you give everyone access,
no one values it.
When you give the wrong people time,
the right people go unseen.
When you let your availability be unlimited,
your peace becomes the cost.

The Soft Boundary That Changed My Life

Now I say:
"I cannot show up for you
in ways I have not shown up for myself."

This is not selfish.
It is stewardship.
It is maturity.
It is alignment.

My availability is not free.
It is earned through responsibility,
reciprocity,
and respect.

And I give it willingly
only to those who understand
what it costs me.

Chapter 10

RETURNING TO MY FIRST LOVE

There is a kind of exhaustion that sleep cannot fix.
A kind of emptiness no relationship can fill.
A kind of hunger no success, no compliment,
no moment of pleasure can satisfy.

It is the exhaustion that comes from being disconnected
from the One who created you.
It is the emptiness that forms
when you stop seeking the One who knows you.
It is the hunger that grows
when you try to replace God
with anything else—
money, people, validation, escape.

For a long time,
I didn't realize I was spiritually starving.
I thought I was just tired.
I thought life was supposed to feel heavy.
I thought wanting more was greed,
and needing more was weakness.

But the deeper truth was this:
I was living outside of the alignment
my soul was designed for.

The Apology I Never Knew I Needed to Make

One of the hardest prayers I ever prayed was this:

"God, I'm sorry."

Not a prayer of guilt—
a prayer of awareness.
A prayer that acknowledged
I had drifted so far
that I no longer recognized myself.

I apologized for chasing money
to fill emotional voids.
For entertaining men
who were never aligned with my future.
For using validation
as a substitute for purpose.

I apologized for losing faith
so deeply
that I began to believe
God would withhold from me
what He had already prepared.

Not because He failed me-
but because I failed to trust
who He is.

That prayer broke something open in me.
It wasn't shame.
It wasn't fear.
It was surrender.

God Was Never Punishing Me

There were moments I felt like God was saying "no"
to everything I prayed for.
But with time,
with maturity,
with clarity,
I learned something sacred:

God doesn't deny you out of cruelty.
He denies you out of protection.

He will not give you anything
you place above Him.
He will not bless you
with what you will idolize.
He will not allow you to keep
what disconnects you from Him.

Some relationships didn't fail-
they were removed.
Some opportunities didn't fall through-
they were blocked.
Some desires didn't manifest-
they were delayed
until I became the woman
who could receive them without losing myself.

God wasn't saying "no" to me.
He was saying:
"Come back."

I Was Afraid to Say Yes to God

Saying yes to God
meant saying no to the world.
No to my habits.
No to my patterns.
No to the versions of myself
that felt fun
but were slowly destroying me.

There were days I didn't want to say yes.
I wanted the comfort of old coping mechanisms,
the thrill of temporary affection,
the distraction of chasing validation,
the illusion of control through sin and self-sabotage.

But every time I chose the world,
the world left me empty.
Every time I chose God,
God led me back to myself.

Faith: The Softest and Strongest Form of Self-Love

Spending time with God
became my lifeline.
Prayer became the place
I learned to breathe again.
Scripture became the place
I learned to see myself clearly.
Stillness became the place
I learned to hear His voice.

And in the quiet,
I realized something that changed my life:

Seeking God was not me reaching for Him.
It was Him reaching for me—
and me finally reaching back.

The Battle Between Who I Was and Who God Called Me to Be

There was a version of me
who operated through fear,
abandonment,
control,
and chaos.

And then there was the version
God kept calling me toward-
the one who walked in peace,
discernment,
patience,
and faith.

Healing required me to choose
which woman would lead my life.

At first, it was a tug-of-war.
The broken version had history.
The healed version had promise.

But God doesn't require perfection-
He requires surrender.
He requires alignment.
He requires willingness.

Every step back to Him
was a step back to myself.
Every "yes" to Him
was a "no" to everything
that no longer aligned with who I was becoming.

Returning to Myself Was Returning to God

As I healed, I realized:
I never lost myself.
I drifted.
I disconnected.
I numbed.
I survived.

But I was never lost—
just waiting.
Waiting for peace.
Waiting for clarity.
Waiting for direction.
Waiting for my heart to soften.

God did not restore me by force.
He restored me by invitation.
By reminding me
who I am,
who I am not,
and who I have always been to Him.

And slowly,
patiently,
faithfully,
I returned.

Not to the girl I was,
but to the woman
He knew I could become.

Part III | Healing

I am not her anymore.
But I honor her.
I am not the lessons alone.
But I carry them.

I am the healed version—
not perfect,
but present.
Not unbreakable,
but unshakeable.
Not untouched by pain,
but unruled by it.

I am the woman who:

walks in peace

speaks with intention

loves with discernment

holds boundaries without apology

prays with expectation

trusts God with the unknown

chooses herself without guilt

stands firm in truth

values her energy

protects her heart

honors her growth

I am not who I used to be.
I am not only who I am now.
I am the bridge between the two—
the product of pain
and the promise of healing.

I am the proof
that evolution is holy,
that identity can be rewritten,
that brokenness can become beauty,
that God restores in layers,
and that a new version of yourself
is always waiting
on the other side of surrender.

I have decided that I am worth keeping
She survived.
I healed.
Now, I live.

She cried.
I learned.
Now, I understand.

She hoped.
I grew.
Now, I believe.

She wanted love.
I became love.
Now, I receive love.

She broke.
I rebuilt.
Now, I rise.

I move forward with her behind me,
lessons within me,
and God ahead of me.

I am not finished.
I am becoming.
And becoming
is the most beautiful thing
I have ever done.

Chapter 11

WHERE THE SILENCE WENT

Silence used to be the place where I lost myself.

The space where doubt grew louder,

where insecurity multiplied,

where my wounds replayed their stories

until I believed them again.

But healed silence is different.

Healed silence is sacred.

It is no longer the echo of abandonment—

it is the sound of alignment.

Healing did not remove the quiet.

It transformed it.

It taught me how to inhabit my own stillness

without fear of what I might find there.

Because now, when the silence comes,

I know exactly where it goes—

into clarity, not confusion.

Into truth, not turmoil.

Into presence, not panic.

Silence Stopped Being Punishment

There was a time when silence felt like rejection.

If someone didn't choose me,

it meant something was wrong with me.

If someone distanced themselves,

it meant I wasn't enough.

If someone overlooked me,

it confirmed my invisibility.

But healing flipped the narrative.

Now, silence is not abandonment—

it is discernment.

It is space created by God

to remove the noise

so I can hear what truly matters.

Silence is where God teaches me

what chaos kept hidden.

The Quiet Truths That Healed Me

In the healed silence,

I began hearing truths

I had been too busy,

too overwhelmed,

too wounded

to recognize before:

"You were never meant to fit in."

Isolation wasn't rejection—

it was protection.

God separated me even in my darkness

to keep me from attaching to what would break me further.

"You don't need to be like her."

Comparison is loud,

but God's voice is steady:

I don't want their reflection.

I want yours.

"No one will choose me."

I used to whisper this in fear.

Now I answer back in strength:

God chose me first.

And I choose myself next.

"I don't want to be without them."

The healed me replies:

I don't want to be without me.

Silence Taught Me How to Love Myself

There is a kind of self-love

you can only hear in the quiet.

Not the soft, pretty kind—

the honest kind.

The kind that says:

"You deserve reciprocity."

"You deserve tenderness."

"You deserve truth."

"You deserve accountability."

"You deserve peace."

And the most transformative:

"You deserve you."

Because for so long,

I abandoned myself to be held by others.

Now, I hold myself

so I never have to abandon me again.

Silence Became My Boundary

Silence is now the place

where I decide who gets access.

Where I evaluate behavior, not excuses.

Where I separate intention from impact.

Where I choose what aligns

and release what does not.

I do not raise my voice anymore.

I do not chase clarity.

I do not negotiate my worth.

I let silence speak for me.

It tells people who I am

and who I will no longer be.

If someone can only hear me

when I am angry or masculine or broken,

they will not hear me at all.

If someone thrives off chaos,

my peace will be the thing that removes me.

If someone only values me in crisis,

my calm will end the connection.

Silence Is Where My Confidence Lives Now

I used to beg to be seen.

Beg to be loved.

Beg to be chosen.

Now, I simply reveal who I am—

and whoever cannot value it

removes themselves by default.

The healed silence is not empty.

It is full:

Full of discernment.

Full of God.

Full of inner authority.

Full of alignment.

Full of peace.

Where the Silence Did Not Go

It didn't disappear.

It evolved.

It shifted from being a void

to being a voice.

It no longer swallows me—

it grounds me.

It no longer drains me—

it restores me.

It no longer isolates me—

it identifies me.

Silence became the room

where the healed version of me

finally stepped forward.

And for the first time in my life,

I am not afraid of the quiet.

I am at home in it.

Chapter 12

LOVING MYSELF OUT LOUD

There was a time when loving myself felt impossible-
a distant concept reserved for women
who had more confidence,
more beauty,
more certainty,
more worth.

I thought self-love was a reward
you earned after becoming perfect.
After healing everything.
After fixing yourself.
After proving your value.

But loving myself out loud
did not come after I became whole-
it's the very thing that made me whole.

Self-Love Was Not a Feeling—It Was a Decision

I didn't wake up one day suddenly confident.
I didn't magically stop criticizing my reflection.
I didn't instantly release my insecurities
just because I knew they were hurting me.

I learned to love myself the same way
I had loved others -
through consistency, compassion, and clarity.

Not through grand gestures,
but through small, sacred decisions:

speaking kindly to myself

refusing to shrink

honoring my boundaries

forgiving myself for what I didn't know then

choosing rest without guilt

leaving relationships that required my suffering

returning to God daily

protecting my peace like it was my home

Every act of self-love
became a brick in the foundation
of the woman I was rebuilding.

The Love Letter That Changed Everything

I once wrote myself a hate letter.
Every insecurity, every wound, every judgment
spilled onto the page.
It was the rawest mirror I had ever held.

But later - years later . . .
I wrote myself a love letter.
And in doing so,
I fell in love with myself
in a way I didn't know was possible.

I wrote to the girl I buried:
I see you now.
I believe you now.
I love you now.

It was the first time
I stopped waiting for someone else
to tell me who I was
and started telling myself.

Choosing Myself Without Apology

For years, I thought choosing myself
meant losing others.
I thought boundaries were selfish.
I thought self-prioritization was arrogance.

But healing taught me this:
If choosing yourself threatens a relationship,
the relationship was built on your self-neglect.

I no longer apologize for prioritizing my peace.
For saying no.
For needing space.
For choosing solitude over chaos.
For leaving when I feel God pulling me away.
For protecting the softness I worked so hard to reclaim.

Loving myself out loud
means letting my life reflect my worth-
not in perfection,
but in alignment.

Letting Go of Being Overlooked

I used to crave being chosen.
I used to hope someone would finally see me,
finally value me,
finally cherish me.

But the healed version of me knows:
If someone cannot recognize my worth,
it is because they were never meant to carry it.

Self-love turned rejection
into redirection.
It turned loneliness
into preparation.
It turned abandonment
into elevation.

I stopped begging for love.
I stopped performing for affection.
I stopped proving myself to people
who benefitted from my brokenness.

Now, I simply show up—
whole, present, aligned.
And whoever is meant for me
will recognize the language of peace I speak.

Loving Myself Through God

God didn't heal me
by giving me everything I wanted.
He healed me
by teaching me who I am.

His love became the blueprint
for how I learned to love myself:

Unconditionally.
Patiently.
Truthfully.
Without abandoning myself in the process.

Now my self-love is not rooted
in appearance, relationships, or achievements-
it is rooted in identity.
In knowing that I am chosen,
cherished,
designed with intention.

Loving Myself Out Loud Means Living Out Loud

No more shrinking.
No more apologizing.
No more silencing my truth
to keep others comfortable.

I am allowed to take up space.
I am allowed to speak boldly.
I am allowed to change.
I am allowed to be proud of myself.
I am allowed to walk away.
I am allowed to glow.

Loving myself out loud
does not mean announcing my growth
it means embodying it.
It means living in a way
that honors the healed woman I am becoming.

I am no longer waiting
to be loved the way I love.
I am giving that love
to myself first.

And from that fullness,
everything else flows.

Chapter 13

BECOMING THE WOMAN, I NEEDED

There comes a moment in every healing journey
when you stop waiting for someone to save you
and finally realize-
you are the person you've been waiting for.

For years, I longed for a woman I had never met:
a version of myself who was strong but soft,
wise but teachable,
loving but discerning,
whole but still growing.

I imagined her.
Prayed for her.
Chased her.
Punished myself for not being her.

And then one day,
I understood the truth:
I wasn't supposed to find her.
I was supposed to become her.

The Woman I Needed Set Standards Without Apology

She didn't lower her boundaries
to make others feel comfortable.
She didn't tolerate disrespect
and call it loyalty.
She didn't justify bad behavior
because she saw potential.
She didn't silence herself
just to be chosen.

She spoke clearly.
Loved deeply.
Walked away gracefully.
Grew consistently.
Prayed without ceasing.

She didn't beg.
She didn't chase.
She didn't shrink.
She didn't settle.

She lived in truth,
even when it cost her company.
She honored her worth,
even when others overlooked it.
She protected her peace,
even when people called her distant.

She was everything
I didn't know I was allowed to be.

I am everything I was afraid to become.

The Woman I Needed Didn't Fear Solitude

For so long, I feared being alone.
I equated solitude with abandonment,
quiet with rejection,
distance with unworthiness.

But the healed woman in me
understands solitude differently.

Solitude is alignment.
Solitude is clarity.
Solitude is where God speaks
without interruption.

The woman I needed
was not afraid to stand alone—
because she knew she was never standing alone.
God stood with her.
Purpose stood with her.
Peace stood with her.

She understood that losing people
is often how God makes room.

The Woman I Needed Chose Responsibility Over Excuses

She didn't hide behind trauma.
She acknowledged it.
She didn't repeat old patterns.
She studied them.
She didn't blame others
for the choices she made-
she held herself accountable
and grew from it.

She didn't just admit her wrongs.
She corrected them.
She didn't just break cycles.
She replaced them with healthier ones.

She moved differently
because she understood differently.

The Woman I Needed Walked with God Fully, Not Partially

The broken version of me loved God
from a distance.
The healed version of me
loves Him in surrender.

The woman I needed
didn't run to God only in crisis-
she walked with Him daily.
Her peace came from His presence.
Her confidence came from His promises.
Her identity came from His truth.

She no longer prayed from fear.
She prayed from faith.
She no longer prayed to survive.
She prayed to transform.

The Woman I Needed Stopped Abandoning Herself

I used to betray myself
just to be loved.
I used to silence myself
just to be accepted.
I used to hurt myself
to keep others happy.

But the woman I needed
does not do that.
She will not lose herself
to keep anyone.
She will not settle
to avoid loneliness.
She will not leave herself unseen
to keep someone else comfortable.

She knows her value.
She honors her emotions.
She listens to her intuition.
She respects her limits.

And when something or someone
no longer aligns,
she leaves-
without chaos,
without guilt,
without looking back.

The Woman I Needed Is the Woman I Am Becoming

I am not perfect.
I am not finished.
I am not healed all the way through.

But I am growing into the woman
I once prayed for.
I am learning to show up
as the healed version of myself,
not the wounded one.

Every boundary I set
is a promise kept to myself.
Every truth I tell
is a layer of armor removed.
Every moment of peace I choose
is a step closer to her.

I am becoming the woman
who loves without losing herself,
who gives without depleting herself,
who heals without hiding from the truth,
who stands firm without becoming hard,
who trusts God without conditions,
who honors herself without apology.

She is no longer a fantasy.
She is no longer a distant dream.
She is no longer a version of me
I feel unworthy of.

She is me—
growing,
stretching,
transforming,
aligning,
becoming.

And I am proud of her.

Chapter 14

WHEN DREAMS CHANGE

There is a version of me that believed
dreams must stay the same to be valid.
That if my vision shifted,
if my desires evolved,
if my plan changed-
it meant I failed.

But life taught me something truer:
Dreams are allowed to grow just like I am.
They are allowed to stretch, to shift,
to transform as I transform.
A changed dream is not a dead dream.
It is a dream reborn.

The Old Dream Was Built by a Wounded Version of Me

The dreams I once held
were shaped by survival,
by validation,
by fear,
by who I thought I needed to be
to earn love or stability or respect.

I wanted success
so no one could look down on me.
I wanted money
so I never had to need anyone.
I wanted relationships
that proved I was chosen.
I wanted recognition
to soothe the parts of me
that felt invisible.

Those dreams weren't lies.
They were symptoms-
expressions of a girl trying to heal
without the tools to do so.

As I healed,
the dreams that once kept me alive
became too small for the woman I was becoming.

The Plan Changed Because I Changed

There is a humility in accepting
that the path you once fought for
no longer aligns with the person you're growing into.

Healing taught me that:

Plans are flexible.

Purpose is steady.

Dreams are evolving.

Alignment is everything.

I did not quit.
I recalibrated.
I made room for better.
I allowed God to redirect me
without demanding He explain why.

Obstacles Don't Mean "Stop"

Life did not get easier
just because I healed.
In some ways,
it became harder-
because healed eyes
see obstacles differently.

I used to see obstacles as signs of failure.
Now I see them as invitations to grow.
Every challenge became a mirror.
Every setback became a lesson.
Every closed door became protection.

I stopped asking,
"Why is this happening to me?"
and started asking,
"What is this teaching me?"

And with that shift,
I understood:
Obstacles were not meant to stop me.
They were meant to strengthen me.
To refine me.
To prepare me.

I Will Low Crawl If I Must

Healing did not make me passive.
It made me persistent.

There were days I wanted to give up,
days when nothing made sense,
days when God felt silent,
days when my dreams felt distant,
days when progress felt invisible.

But I made myself a promise:
I will move forward
even if I have to low crawl
my entire way there on broken glass.

Not because I enjoy suffering-
but because I refuse to abandon myself again.
I refuse to quit on the woman I'm becoming.
I refuse to let fear
rewrite a story God already authored.

My movement might be slow.
My progress might be quiet.
My path might be unconventional.

But I am moving.
And God moves with me.

The Dream Changed But My Determination Did Not

I am not committed to the dream I once had.
I am committed to the purpose God placed in me.
Dreams shift.
Purpose stays.

I am allowed to evolve.
I am allowed to start over.
I am allowed to rewrite the plan.
I am allowed to want something new.
I am allowed to outgrow old visions.
I am allowed to dream again
and again
and again.

Healing taught me that the dream
is not the finish line-
it is the becoming.
The journey.
The refinement.
The alignment with who God called me to be.

I didn't quit.
I transformed.
I adjusted.
I surrendered.
I kept going.

I am still going.

And now-
the woman I am becoming
is building dreams
the woman I used to be
never knew she was worthy of.

ABOUT THE AUTHOR

Shannon writes from the space between who she was expected to be and who she became when she finally chose herself.

The Self I Was Yet to Know was born in seasons of quiet unraveling, where clarity replaced performance, boundaries replaced over-explanation, and healing became an active decision rather than a distant goal. Her work reflects the courage it takes to outgrow rooms, relationships, and versions of self that no longer fit.

With a voice rooted in honesty, faith, and self-discipline, Shannon explores identity, purpose, and renewal through lived experience. She believes growth doesn't always look loud. Sometimes it looks like structure, rest, and the audacity to protect your peace.